Leprechaun's Gold

By Alyssa Curtayne
Illustrated By Maria Rask

Dedicated to my grandparents,
who taught me about love.
With much thanks also to
Leanne and George.

On their holiday to the beach
last year, Jess and Abbie brought
back more than sand in their shoes
and happy memories.
Abbie saw him first.
"Look," she pointed.
"Can you see him?"
"I can't see anything but trees," Jess said.
"You don't look with your eyes, Jess,
but with your imagination."

But Jess still couldn't see him.

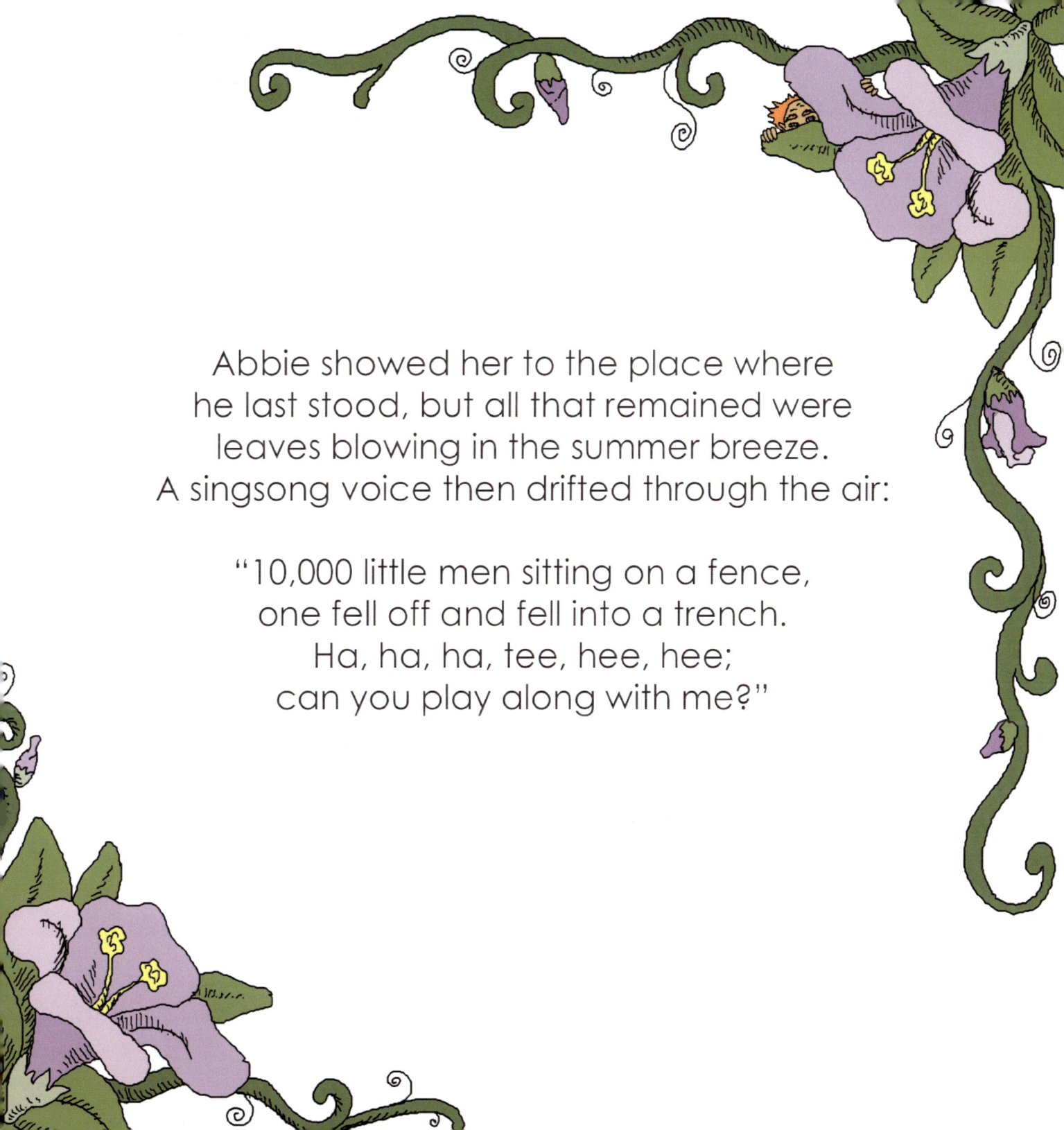

Abbie showed her to the place where
he last stood, but all that remained were
leaves blowing in the summer breeze.
A singsong voice then drifted through the air:

"10,000 little men sitting on a fence,
one fell off and fell into a trench.
Ha, ha, ha, tee, hee, hee;
can you play along with me?"

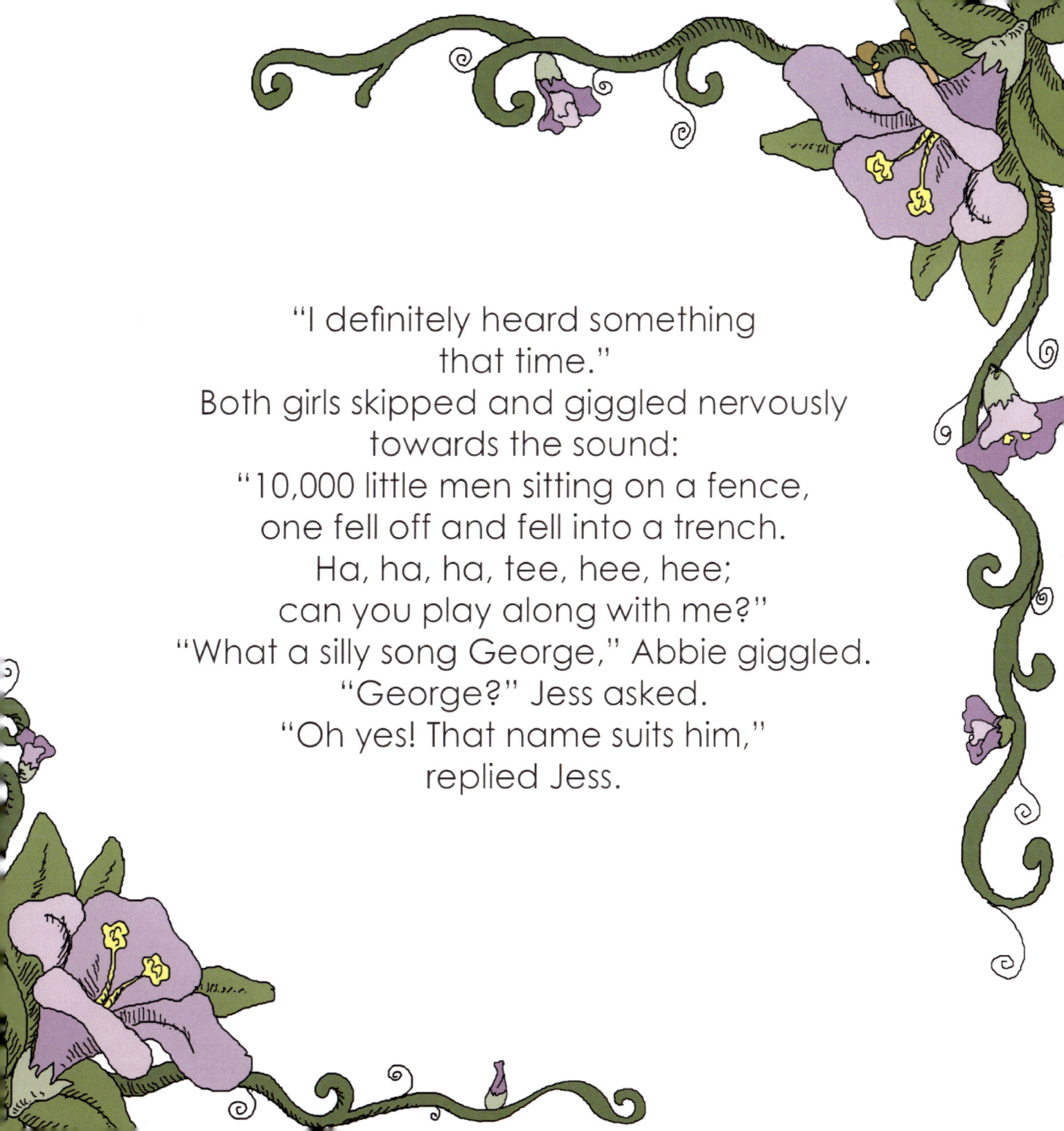

"I definitely heard something
that time."
Both girls skipped and giggled nervously
towards the sound:
"10,000 little men sitting on a fence,
one fell off and fell into a trench.
Ha, ha, ha, tee, hee, hee;
can you play along with me?"
"What a silly song George," Abbie giggled.
"George?" Jess asked.
"Oh yes! That name suits him,"
replied Jess.

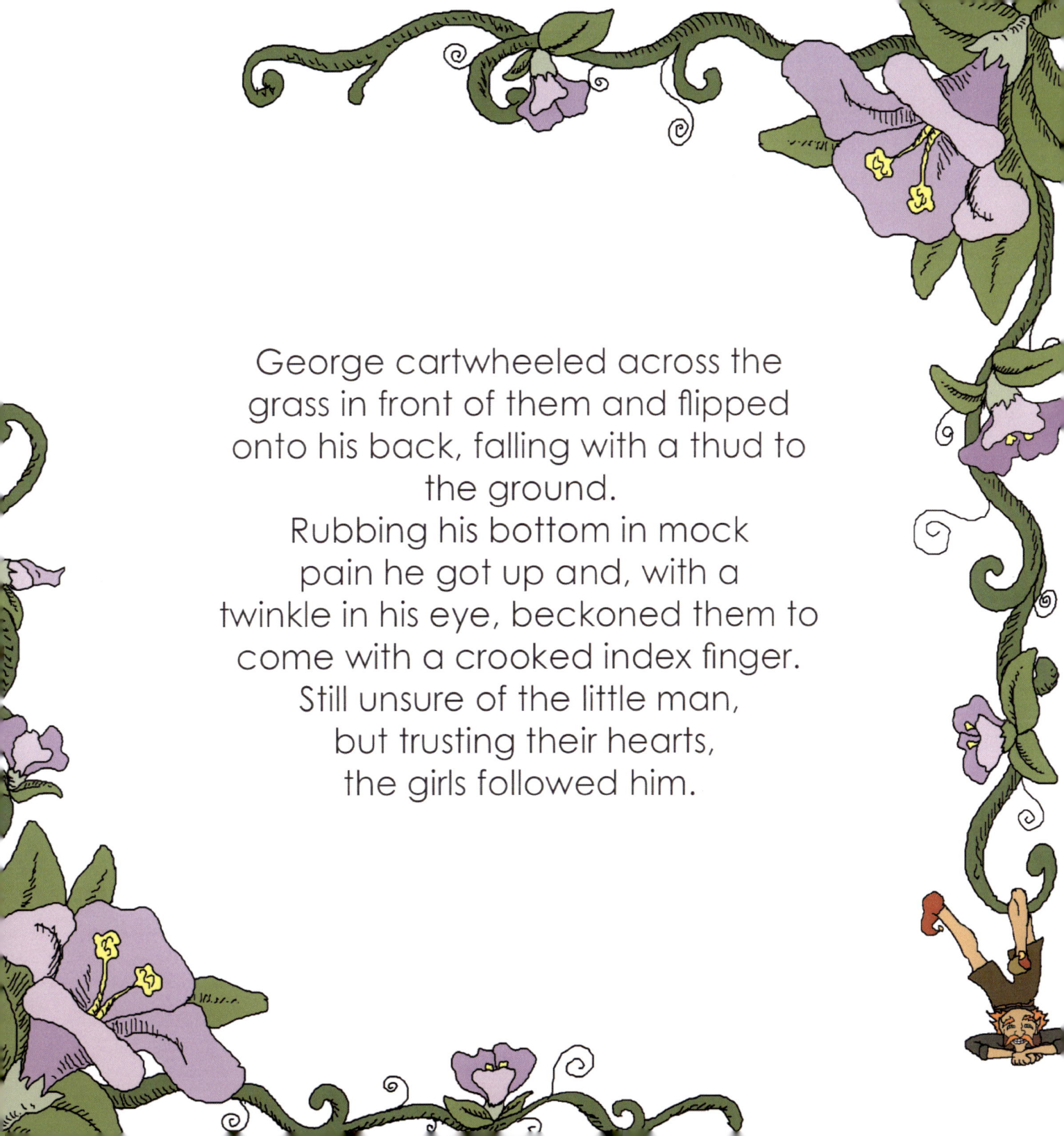

George cartwheeled across the
grass in front of them and flipped
onto his back, falling with a thud to
the ground.
Rubbing his bottom in mock
pain he got up and, with a
twinkle in his eye, beckoned them to
come with a crooked index finger.
Still unsure of the little man,
but trusting their hearts,
the girls followed him.

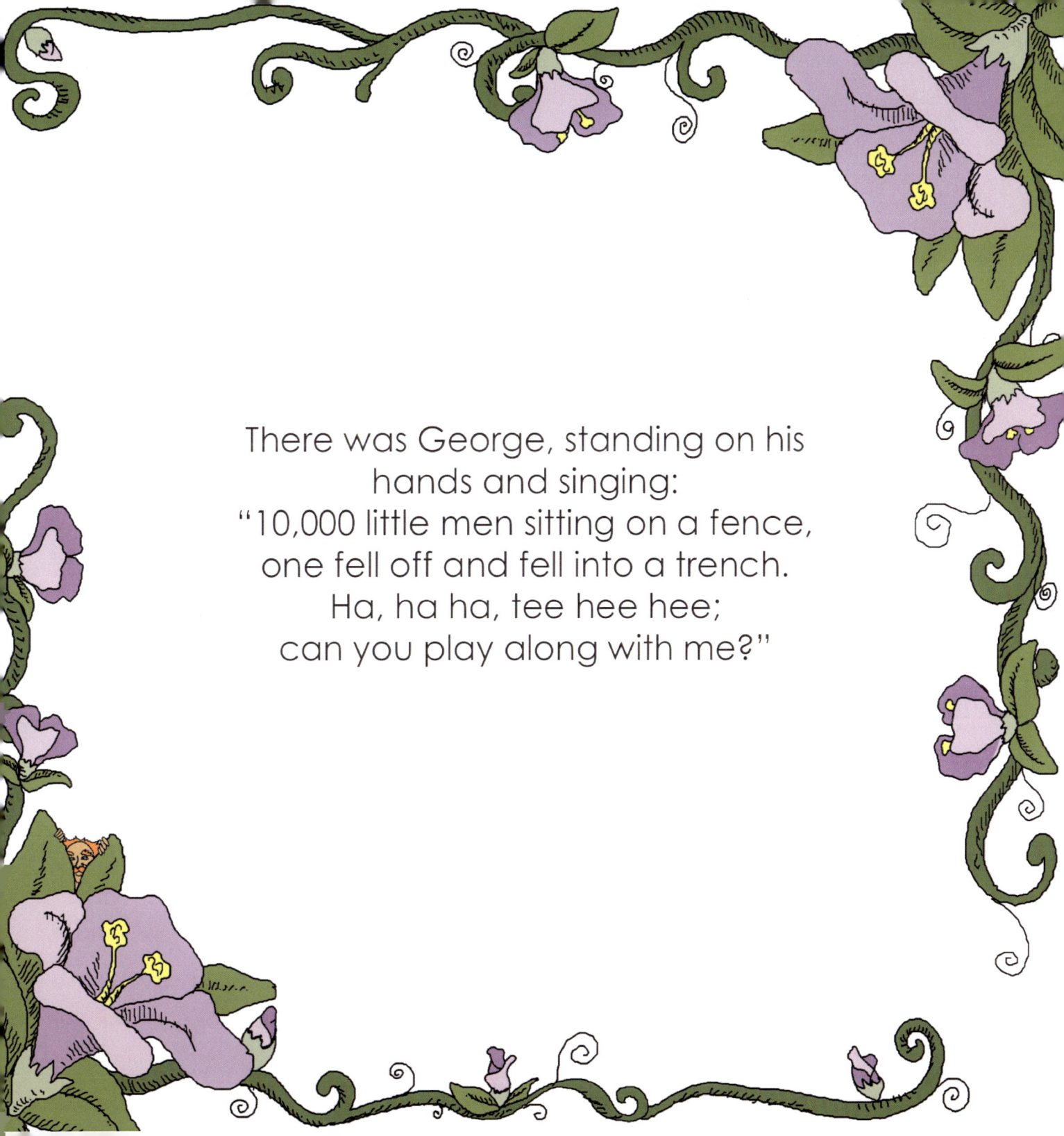

There was George, standing on his
hands and singing:
"10,000 little men sitting on a fence,
one fell off and fell into a trench.
Ha, ha ha, tee hee hee;
can you play along with me?"

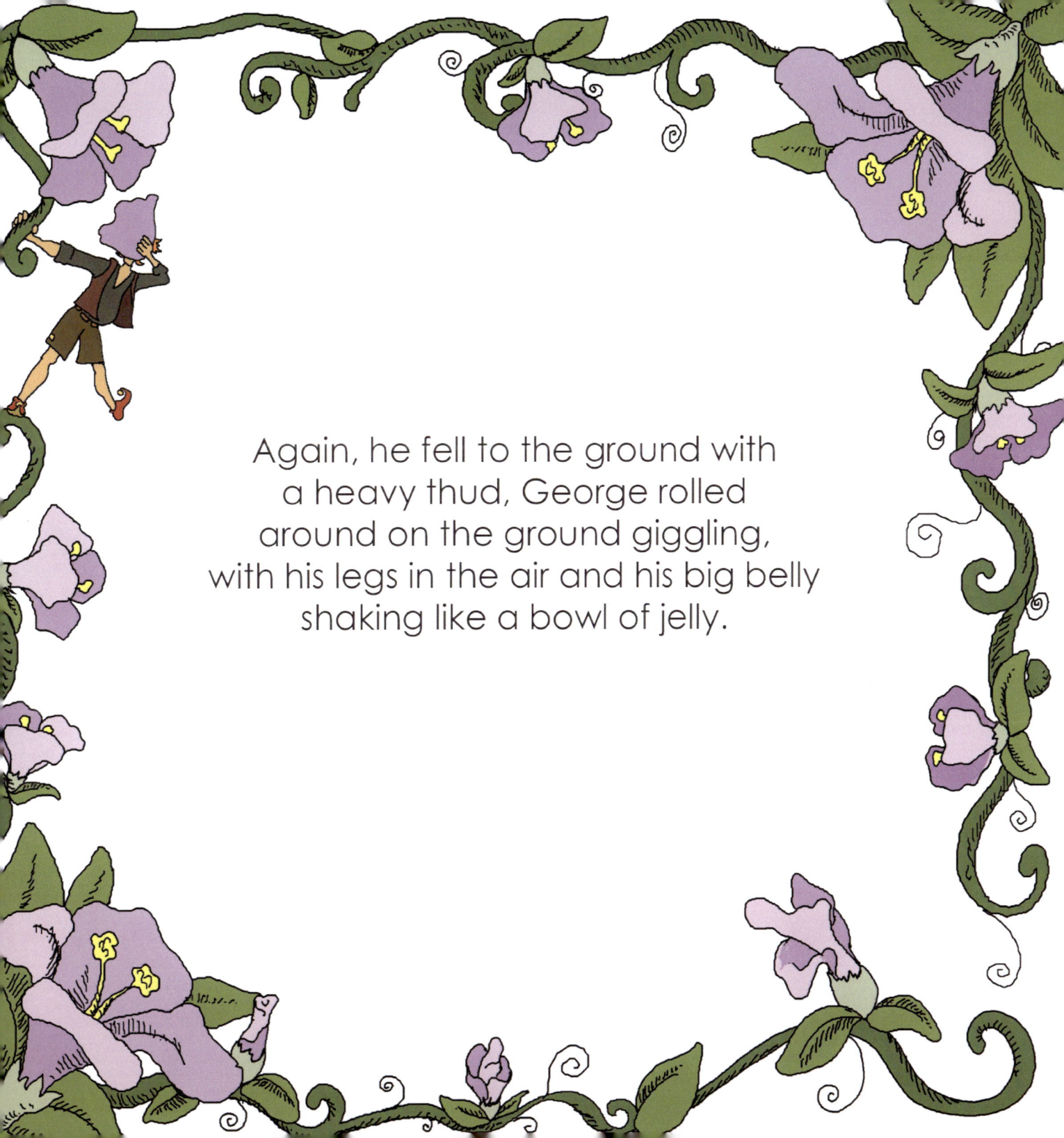

Again, he fell to the ground with
a heavy thud, George rolled
around on the ground giggling,
with his legs in the air and his big belly
shaking like a bowl of jelly.

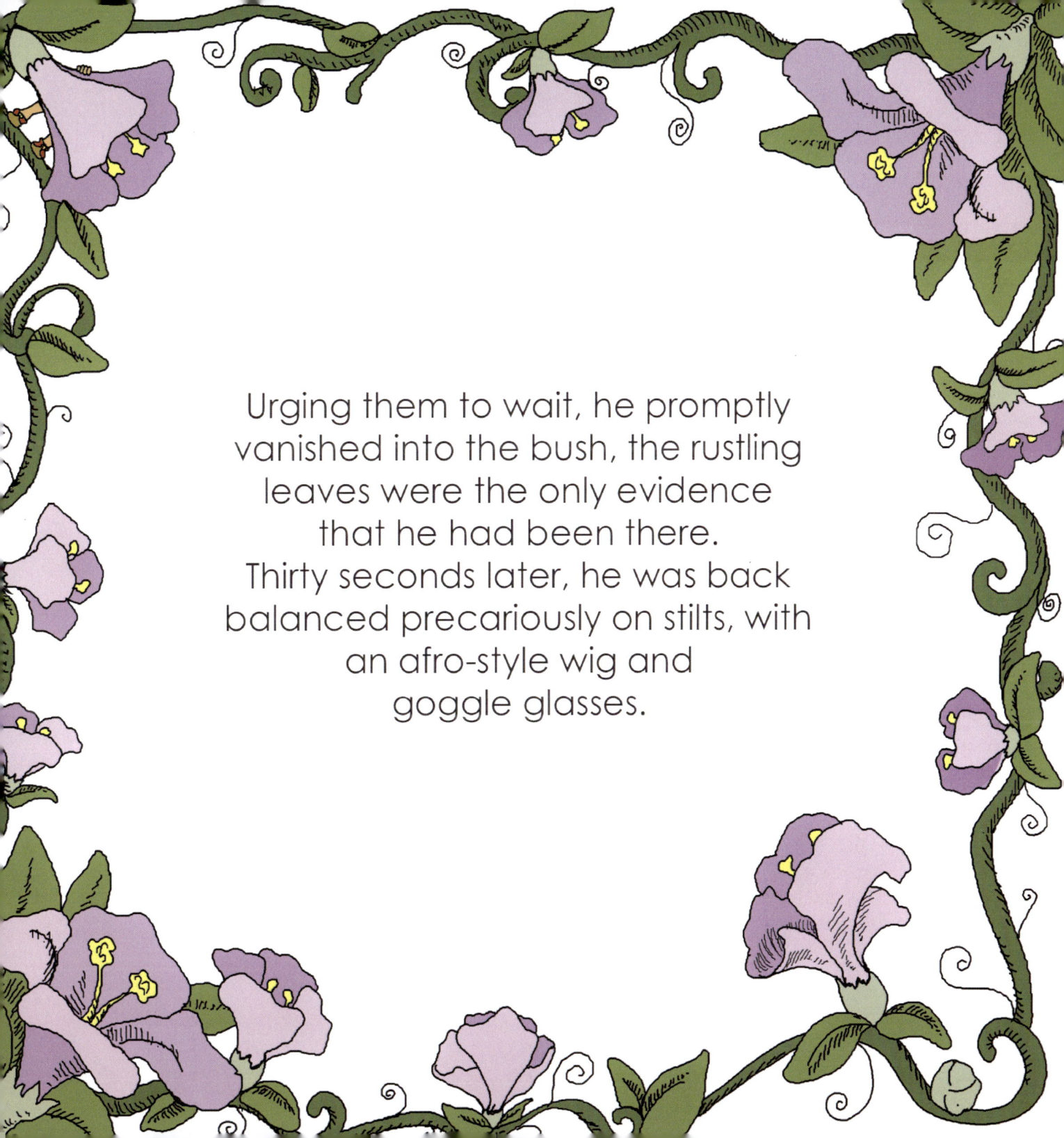

Urging them to wait, he promptly
vanished into the bush, the rustling
leaves were the only evidence
that he had been there.
Thirty seconds later, he was back
balanced precariously on stilts, with
an afro-style wig and
goggle glasses.

George danced to the beat of
a band that wasn't there;
Moon-walking and disco jiving
across the grass.
As the girls danced with him, Jess laughed:
"George, you are the funniest little
fellow on the planet!
Can we take you home with us?
You are so much fun."

The next morning he led them to the beach, where he stood motionless, looking to the sea.

"What's he doing Abbie?" Jess asked.
"Shh, just wait," she replied.

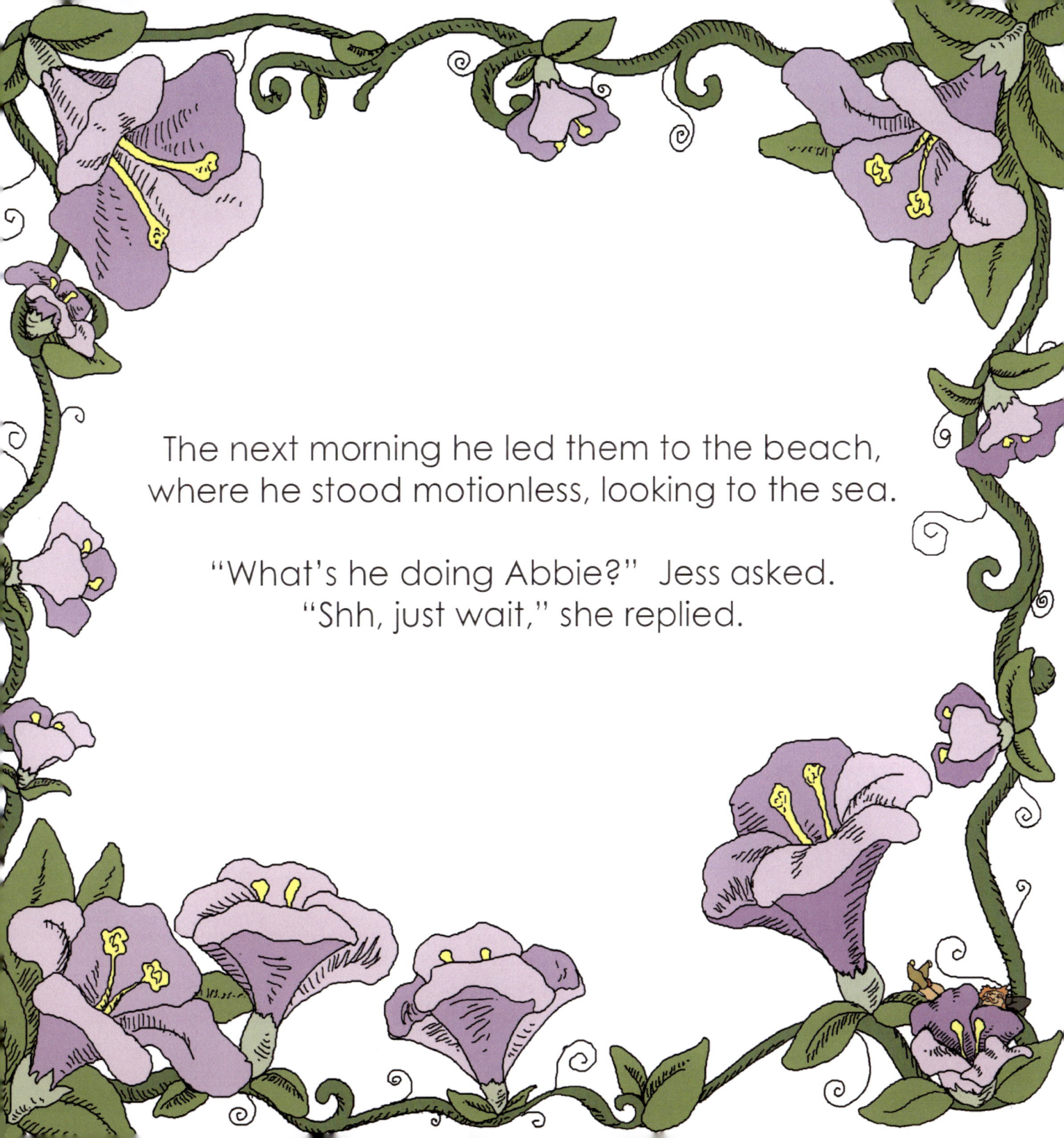

With eyes closed, George raised his
arms to the sky, sang a little song,
and placed his hands on his heart.
Out across the horizon a speck
of colour hovered just
above the water.

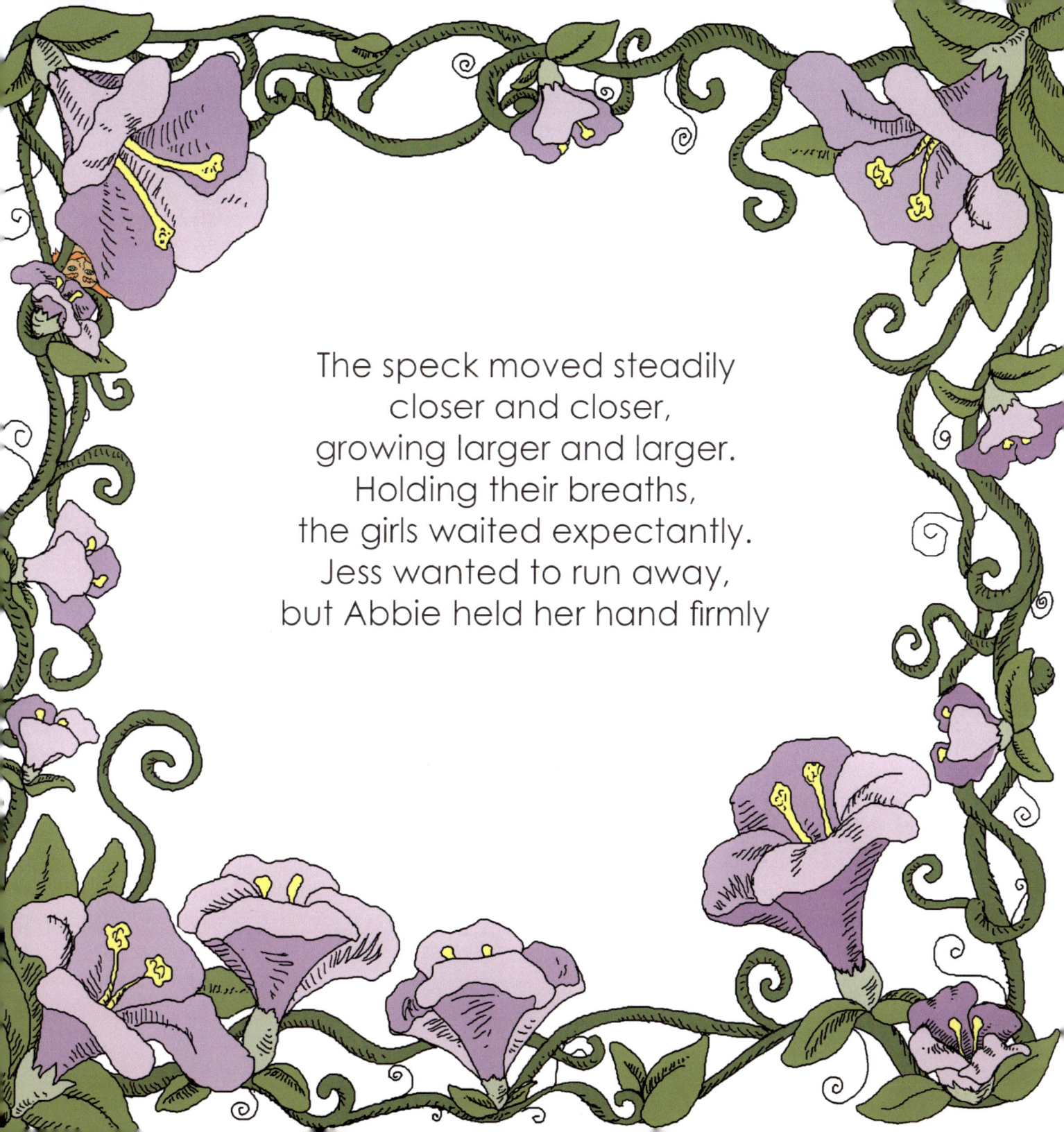

The speck moved steadily
closer and closer,
growing larger and larger.
Holding their breaths,
the girls waited expectantly.
Jess wanted to run away,
but Abbie held her hand firmly

Finally, the colours splashed at their feet and turned into a blazing colour of rainbow that arched across the morning sky.
"Amazing," Jess breathed.

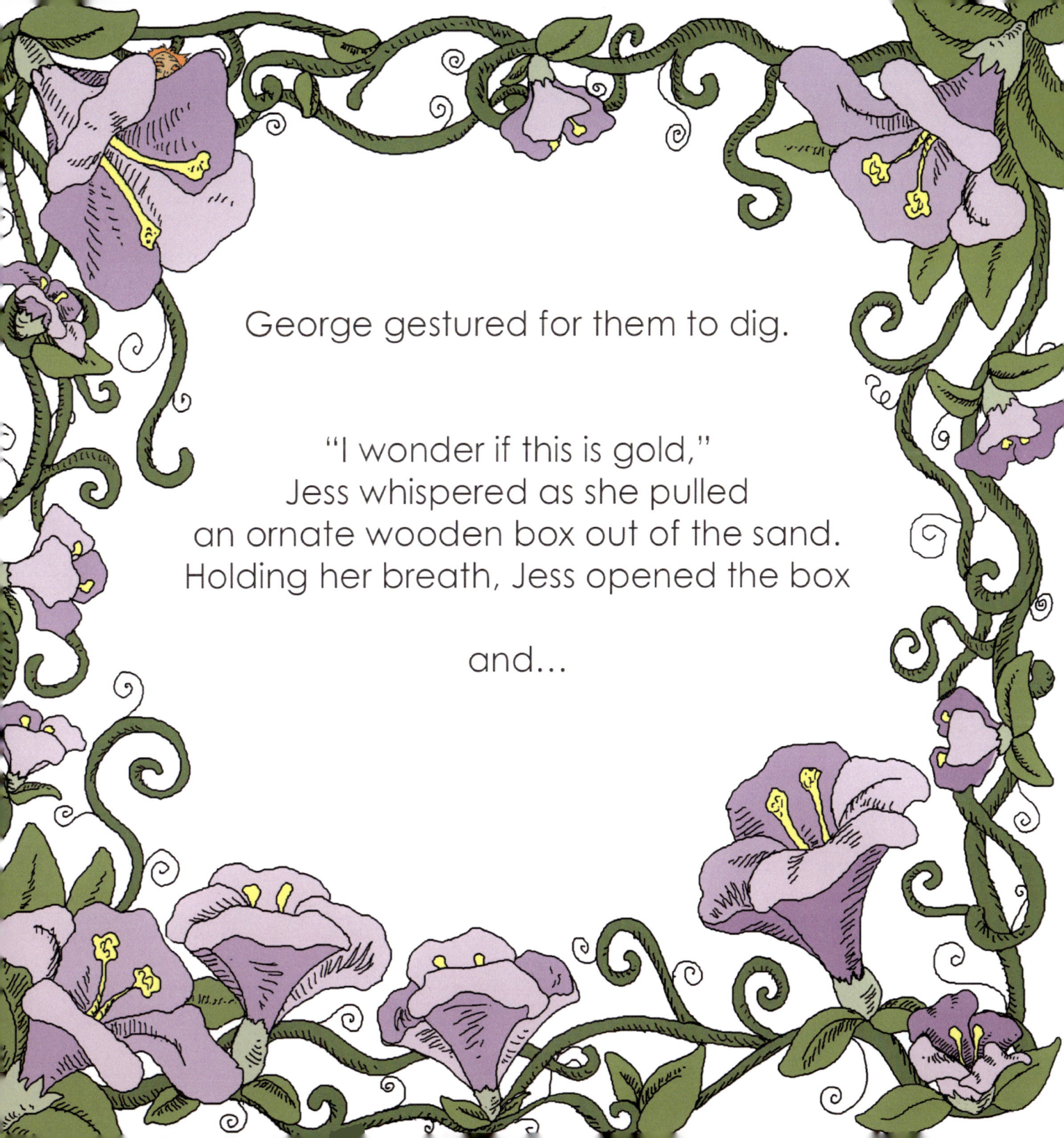

George gestured for them to dig.

"I wonder if this is gold,"
Jess whispered as she pulled
an ornate wooden box out of the sand.
Holding her breath, Jess opened the box

and...

…out poured a shaft of light that flared directly into the sky. Shielding their eyes from it, the girls fell back in surprise.

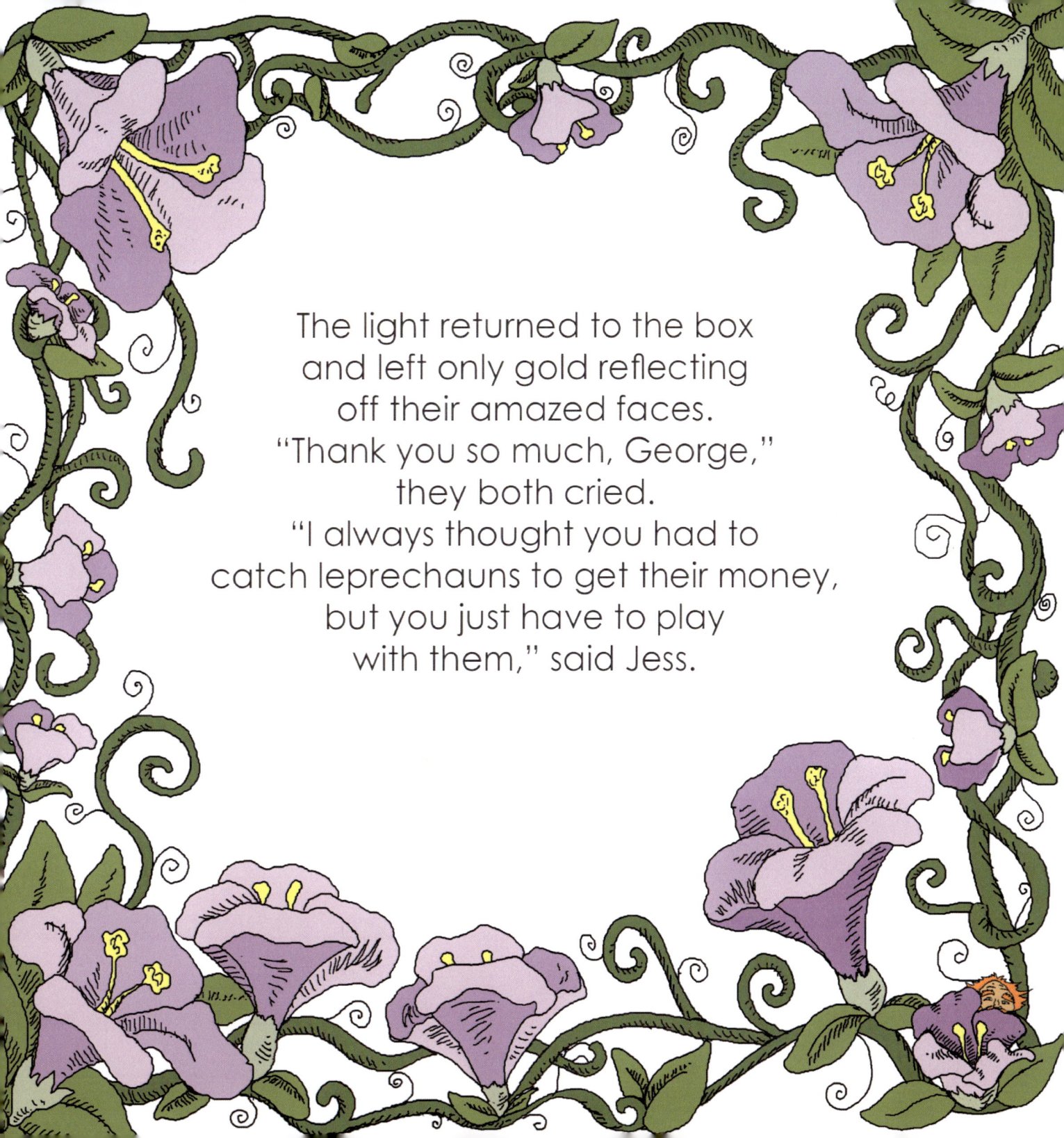

The light returned to the box
and left only gold reflecting
off their amazed faces.
"Thank you so much, George,"
they both cried.
"I always thought you had to
catch leprechauns to get their money,
but you just have to play
with them," said Jess.

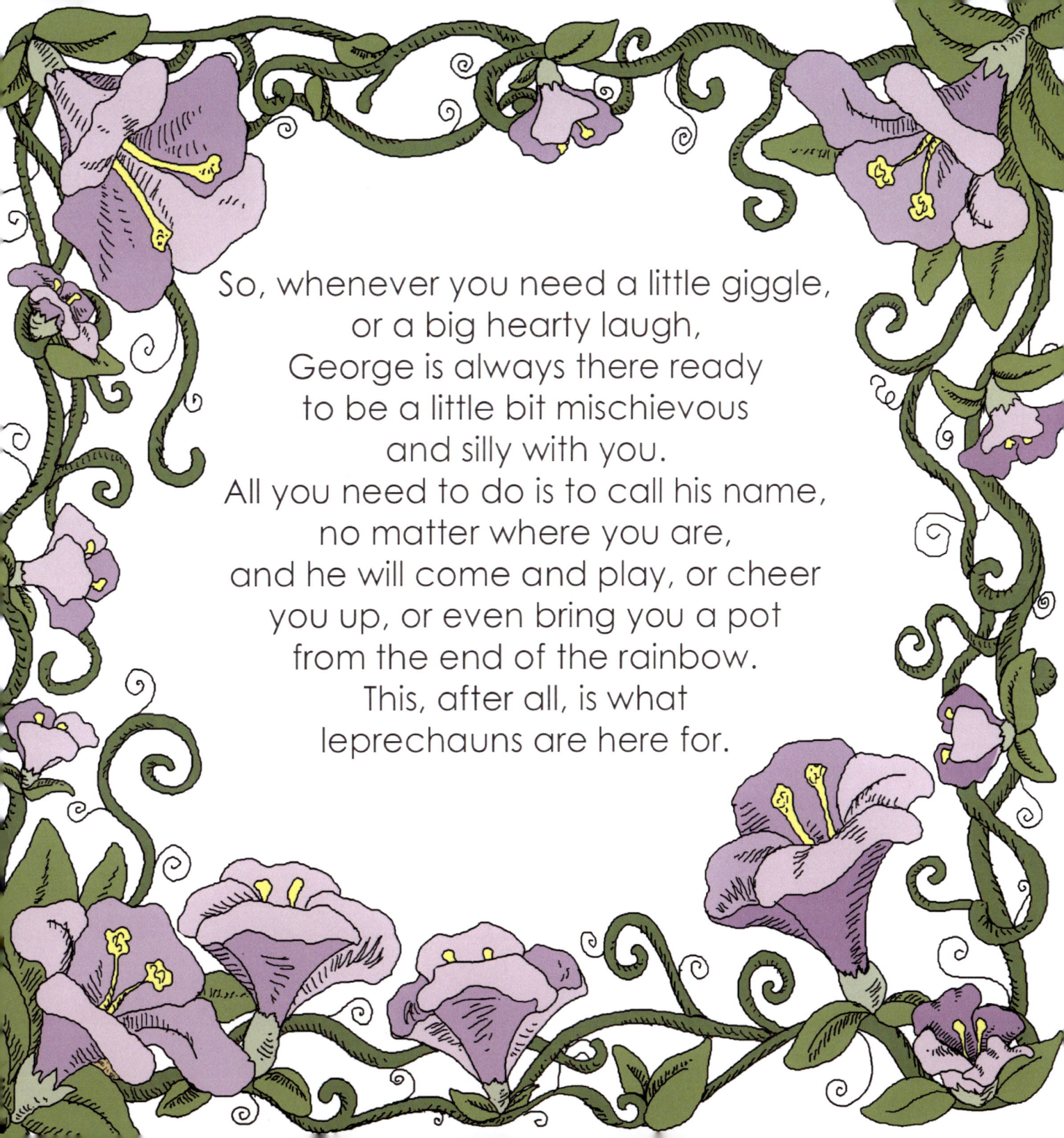

So, whenever you need a little giggle,
or a big hearty laugh,
George is always there ready
to be a little bit mischievous
and silly with you.
All you need to do is to call his name,
no matter where you are,
and he will come and play, or cheer
you up, or even bring you a pot
from the end of the rainbow.
This, after all, is what
leprechauns are here for.

First published by Rising Spirit; Where Great Ideas Grow in 2009 in Tasmania. This edition was published in 2023, in Perth, WA, Australia This edition published in 2023 Copyright ©2009 and ©2023 Alyssa Curtayne

The right of Alyssa Curtayne to be identified as author of this work has been asserted in accordance with the Copyright, Designs and Patents Act 1988.

This publication is copyright. Apart from any use as permitted under the Copyright Act 1968, no part may be reproduced by any process without prior permission from the publisher/author.

www.alyssacurtayne.com

www.ingramcontent.com/pod-product-compliance
Lightning Source LLC
Chambersburg PA
CBRC092340290426
44109CB00008B/168